POETRY PETALS

PAINTED EMOTIONS IN FRAGILE LINES

ISHI SINGLA

Made with ♥ on the Notion Press Platform
www.notionpress.com

To those who find solace in silence, who seek beauty in the mundane, and who discover strength in vulnerability.

For the dreamers, the wanderers, and the lovers of words— may these poems be a gentle companion on your journey, a light in your darkest hours, and a reminder that you are never alone.

With heartfelt gratitude, Ishi Singla

Contents

Preface

Poetry has always been the language of the unsaid—the whispers between heartbeats, the echoes of fleeting moments, and the rhythm of existence itself. This collection is born from such fragments, gathered from the tapestry of life and woven together with words.

Through these poems, you will journey across the landscapes of emotions—joy and sorrow, love and loss, hope and longing. Each verse is a reflection of the world as I see it, yet it seeks to resonate with your own stories and truths.

This is not just a book; it is an invitation. An invitation to pause, to ponder, and to feel deeply. It is a space where the mundane transforms into the magical, where the ordinary reveals its hidden beauty.

I hope that as you turn these pages, you find pieces of yourself in the words, and perhaps, discover new ways to connect with the world and those around you.

1. Beauty in flaws

In every whisper there lie a melodious voice,
In every touch there lie care and affection,
Beauty is everywhere even in the ugliest flaws,
A rough bark, strength it holds;
An ugly painting, lessons it told;
God has made this world as his most beautiful creation,
As we say…
Beauty is in eye of the beholder,
So, if you heart is pure; your sight is holistic, and everything
is beautiful.

2. Thinking of a poetess

This world needs people,
Who find beauty in love,
Elegance in mundane,
And strength in vulnerability.
This world posses some courage; that inspires us too,
There is some magic waiting to be unveiled,
A little patience waiting to be admired,
And a bunch of happiness waiting to be shared…
There is something wonderful about this world, the nature
and the mankind; I believe…
So, explore this world with a positive mind, limitless courage
and unconditional love.

3. Lonely life

In a wild corner, I am sitting alone;

In silent nights, my screaming soul;

In this gloomy world, not even worth a dime;

I know my dullness can never shine.

My ideas are taken, my heart is broken;

My spirit is shivering, blaming itself…

'Every wrong thing is your fault at the end'

My mind knows am not a winner, it knows that I am done with life;

Every second is haunting me, so is every blunt knife;

I don't know what to do?

Never, what to think?

With times pace my heart quickly shrink,

I always knew, my life is hollow;

With every scar, a story follow;

But these odds make me mine,

I know my dullness can never shine…

4. Garden of gemstones

I wondered if it's real, garden of gemstones bright and clear.

Unfolding the mysteries of nature, Let's set out on a journey of dreams and fears.

Days of walking with all my rage, I came across a human race.

Pride and patience was all the sow, in the golden fields their glory glowed.

For a moment if I take a step out.

What a beauty! Still makes me doubt.

Now I see what pain my eyes they are the cities where money is divine.

No love or care for mother or brother, priorities are so cheap I describe.

I just passed through a garden of gemstones all filled with hearts clear and bright.

5. I dreamt a dream which came true

At night on the bed, when I was writhing my head, I dreamt of a world very few people said.

I dreamt of clouds that rained hearts, I dreamt of a world all united as one.

I dreamt of justice falling from the trees, a new life to the poor and an ode to good deeds.

I dreamt of kindness flowing in the rivers, a world where people helped one without any tears.

I dreamt of books fill with joy, a world where people say that happiness may not die.

The world I crept for is now all mine and the love I dreamt of is now divine.

6. In true state of mind

An aimers job is to aim,to go through with the pain

If you are an aimer and you think you can't just don't try and give up at last

If you are an aimer and you think you have lost just go back home and never think a lot

If you are an aimer and you think it's impossible,what a tale too much a predictable

You are an aimer not an astrologer my lad,just focus on your work and let go the bad

Follow your heart,listen what it says,every part of life is a challenge these days

Your life depend on your goals and this is the time to set them or not,so stand up and aim,don't waste your time bcoz soon it will rain

7. Freedom or Loneliness ?

Me in a corner sitting alone,no one to cuddle,no one to hold
No one to give me birthday cards,no one to see all these scars
No one to wish,no one to dance,no one to give me an another chance
No one to hear,no one to dare for my mind filled with these nightnares

8. NOURISHING NATURE

Happiness revolves in my mind when I wake up in the days light,

When birds chirp,it diverts my mind to soothing nature and beauties spite;

I imagine myself in sunflower fields unveiling the nature veiled in green

Valleys green and shimmering streams but my imagination is just a dream.

9. Winter nights

When darkness surrounds,the world around,

A freezing body,a creek sound

Will she find comfort or profound ?

Step 1 and 2 a growling wooh!

Entering gloom,will flowers bloom ?

No,never,struggles so brave,for a new life,she will crave

A lantern in hand the breeze flow shoo!

These freezing winters,what will she do?

A sound sleep or a cup of tea,a cozy blanket or a movie to see.

10. Rain sounds

I saw a raindrop hit my window, I was the one who crept for indoors.
A rhythm to the sound soft and deep , a hit to my window so good it feels…
But the thunder made my blood run cold, I am not the one who will surrender to the dread,
I still hope for some sunshine falling on my bed.
Nightmares in the rain drove me crazy but I still have a room to make me fell cozy.

11. Honesty

A world where dreams come to life, honesty is left a way behind..

As life of a lad, I saw this world ,it grew more bad and bad.

Where lies surround the world with pride the conqueror seems honest why don't we fight .

Lets dwell into the sight of might, let us think what's wrong and what's right.

12. New beginings

Lets rewind the time, when life was tough;
I always needed, more nothing was enough,
Everything had a flaw, but I moved on in truths shadow;
I learned as life flowed ,and with time i brightly glowed;;
With a lesson learnt ,and haunts of past;
I know that hard times end up fast,
With a positive mind and a helping hand ,I am slolwy building my wonderland.

13. Awaiting skies of hope and joy

On a cloudy day,

full of insult and unexpessed pain, a hope so strong to lead my way;

A breath of hurt, a sigh of fear;

Hold it true,near and dear;

As it is the joy where life abides,the pleasure of trying,in nervousness,oh dying

The clouds drifted,they set apart a ray of sunshine,a gentle spark

Now,let us gaze at the sunlit sky and fill our hearts with hope and joy

Plans for the future and love for today,a simple smile,a perfect day

A giggle so soft,time slipped like sand when joy held my hand

The year is full of rains and storms,but cherish today

When wonders stared,hope and joy led my way.

14. Hard times

The times when life is just as grave;
People ask me to be brave;
but what do you expect from my heart to hide;
my tears,loneliness,and that fake smile;
no i can't, no i won't;
Thats my strength please never say don't
it's not weak to cry,
it's not ok to die of hard times torture that will soon dry...
so gather your strength, gather your pride,
feelings are not meant to hide,
hard times will end , good times will come
when the dawn turns to dusk...

15. Blackout emotions

In the glory of night,
when stardust takes over
people feel peace a little akward,
but take pity on me the moon and the stars;
I am a bit upset after the days remarks...
I struggled to be the best which people feel useless,
but borrow my heart, borrow my mind
live with a faded smile simmilar to mine,
be fake, as still as alake
the one who drowns all sadness,
and bears the pain untold,
try and live the life of me,
the happy girl you always see...

Thanks For Reading!

"Poetry Petals" is born from such moments—moments of introspection, of fleeting emotions captured in the delicate embrace of words. This collection is a testament to the power of poetry to illuminate the hidden corners of our hearts and minds, to articulate the ineffable, and to connect us in our shared humanity.

The poems within these pages have been inspired by a multitude of experiences: the tender beauty of nature, the profound depths of love and loss, the joys of discovery, and the sorrows of farewell. Each verse is a reflection of a moment in time, a piece of my journey, and an invitation for you to find your own meaning within the lines.

As you read, I hope you allow yourself to linger in the spaces between the words, to feel the rhythm of the verses, and to let the imagery wash over you. Poetry is not just about understanding; it is about feeling. It is my deepest wish that this book resonates with you on an emotional level, offering solace, inspiration, and perhaps even a touch of magic.

Thank you for opening these pages and stepping into this world of words. May "Poetry Petals" be a companion to you in moments of reflection, a source of comfort in times of need, and a reminder of the beauty that exists in every breath.

9 7 9 8 8 9 7 7 7 0 1 7 5